The Garden

A Story of True Love

Pamela Ann Rice

To request permission, contact publisher at info@papercrownmedia.com.

Scripture quotations taken from the (NASB®) New American Standard Bible®, Copyright © 1960, 1971, 1977, 1995, 2020 by The Lockman Foundation. Used by permission. All rights reserved. lockman.org

Scripture quotations marked MSG are taken from The Message, copyright © 1993, 2002, 2018 by Eugene H. Peterson. Used by permission of NavPress. All rights reserved. Represented by Tyndale House Publishers.

Illustrations created by Meliza Farndell using Midjourney AI

ISBN 978-1-7385716-5-9
Published by Paper Crown Publishing

PAPER
CROWN
PUBLISHING

Paper Crown Media Ltd
71-75 Shelton Street
Covent Garden
London
WC2H 9JQ
www.papercrownmedia.com

For those lost in the suffering, confusion, and pains of life.

You are loved more than you know.

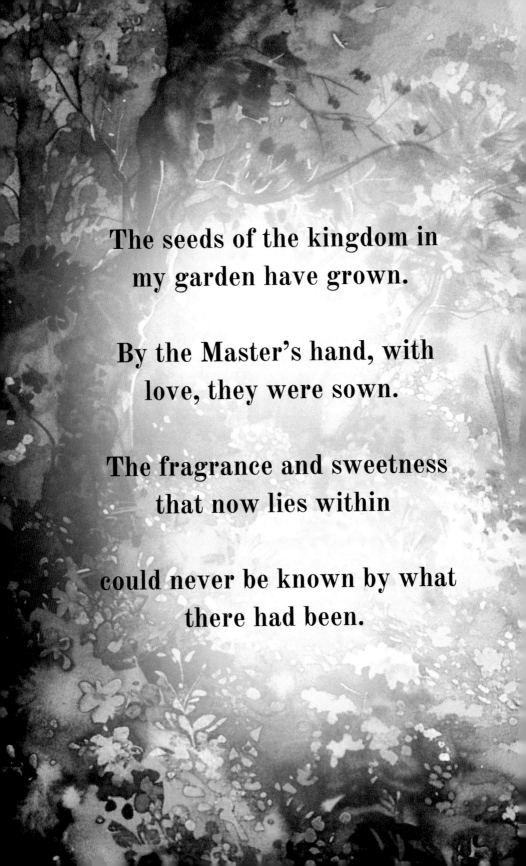

The seeds of the kingdom in
my garden have grown.

By the Master's hand, with
love, they were sown.

The fragrance and sweetness
that now lies within

could never be known by what
there had been.

My hidden garden was
locked up for years.

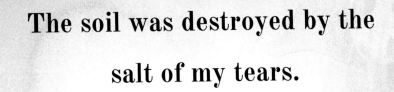

The soil was destroyed by the
salt of my tears.

All that was beautiful died
long ago.

Weeds and thistles were all
that could grow.

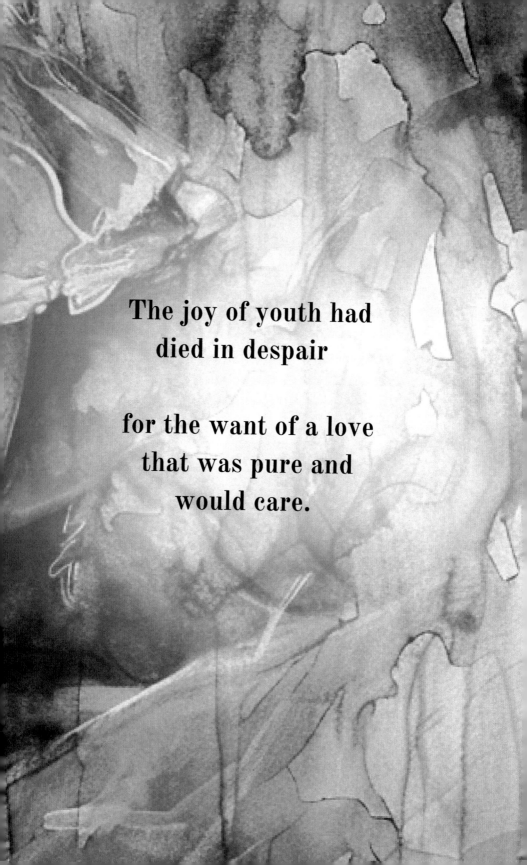

The joy of youth had
died in despair

for the want of a love
that was pure and
would care.

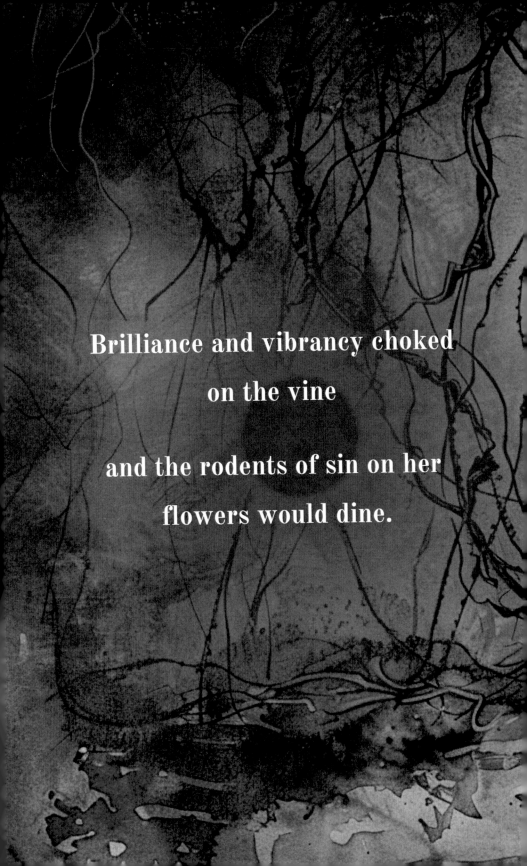

Brilliance and vibrancy choked

on the vine

and the rodents of sin on her

flowers would dine.

The fountain dried up and left
only mud.
The rosebush gave forth not
one little bud.

The grass turned to brown,
and the trees had no leaves,

If anyone saw it, their heart
would just grieve.

My hidden garden so rich
and so rare,

was withered and empty
and totally bare.

The robbers, who raped her,
left her and fled.

Slowly she closed up
until she was dead.

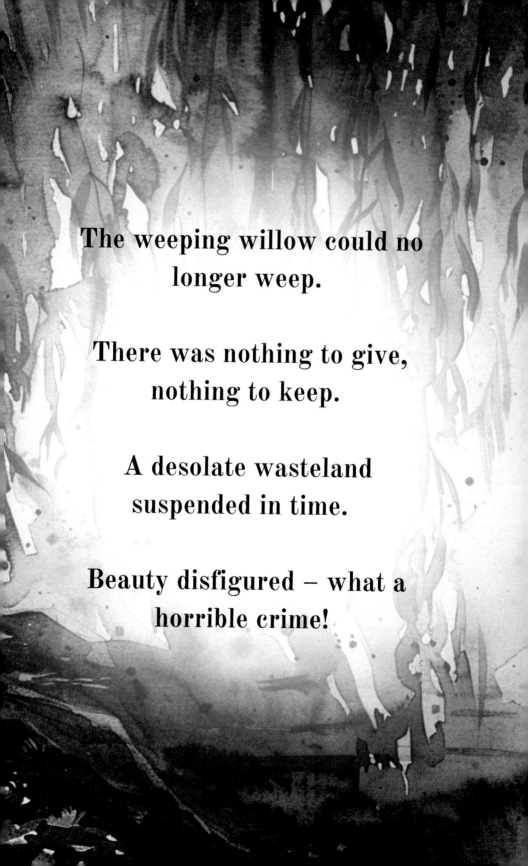

The weeping willow could no
longer weep.

There was nothing to give,
nothing to keep.

A desolate wasteland
suspended in time.

Beauty disfigured – what a
horrible crime!

But Justice appeared...

as the Gardener of Love,

and rained down His Spirit
from heaven above.

He watered the dryness and
softened the ground,

preparing the way for His
grace to abound.

He pulled out the weeds
of broken mistrust,

and burned up the roots
of betrayal and lust.

He raked up anger, rejection, and fear,
until the ground was totally cleared.

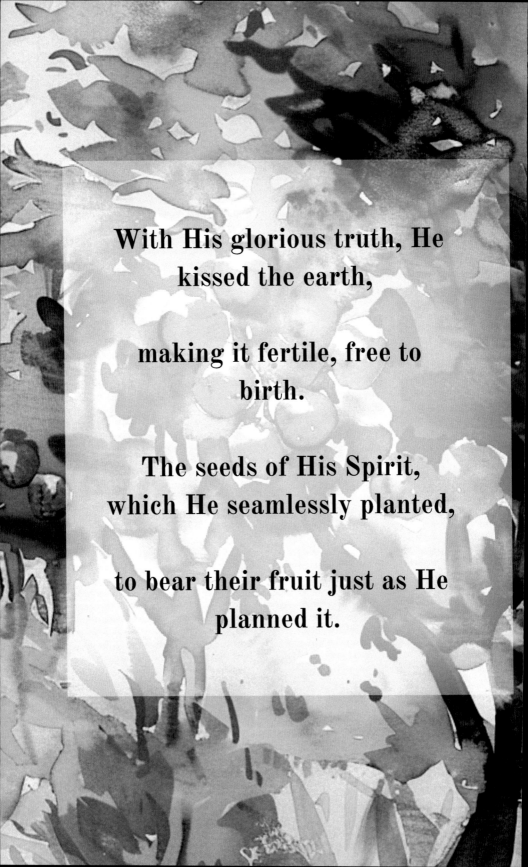

With His glorious truth, He kissed the earth,

making it fertile, free to birth.

The seeds of His Spirit, which He seamlessly planted,

to bear their fruit just as He planned it.

He tended my garden
with watchful eyes,
and rooted out evil and
all of its lies.

With careful attention to
detail He planned,
designing a garden unique
from this land.

Nothing escaped the touch
of the Master.

He was bringing new life
to an utter disaster.

He patiently waited for
His seeds to grow,

protecting their life in
each furrowed row.

The angels in heaven
looked down on His labors,

excitedly telling all of their
neighbors.

They surrounded the garden in
amazement and wonder.

Their wings were so thick it
sounded like thunder.

All the world was waiting to see

what the Gardener of Love
would create her to be.

Could He heal her deep wounds
and revive her heart?

Could He teach her to love and
reveal where to start?

The fountain sprang forth
with clear, living water,

singing a song of love to
His daughter.

As the water flowed, the
garden turned green.

Such a brilliant color had
never been seen.

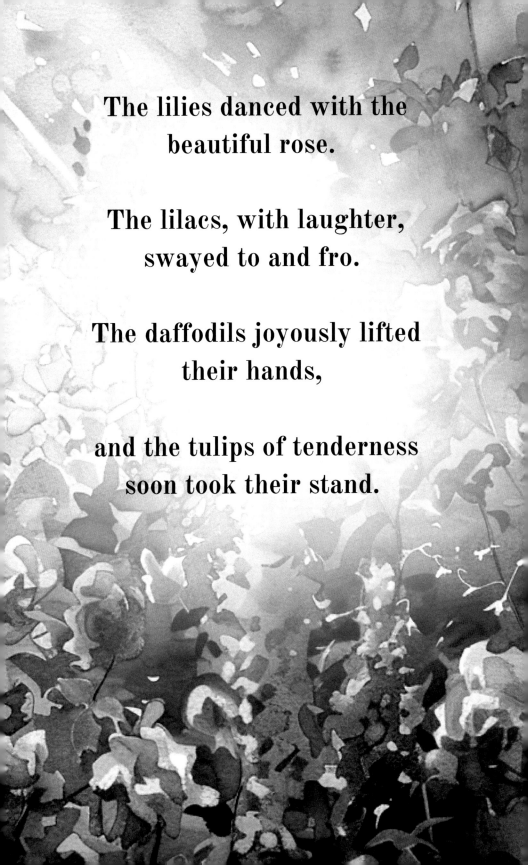

The lilies danced with the
beautiful rose.

The lilacs, with laughter,
swayed to and fro.

The daffodils joyously lifted
their hands,

and the tulips of tenderness
soon took their stand.

The trees all returned to
their powerful stance.

The songbird flew back to
sing on their branch.

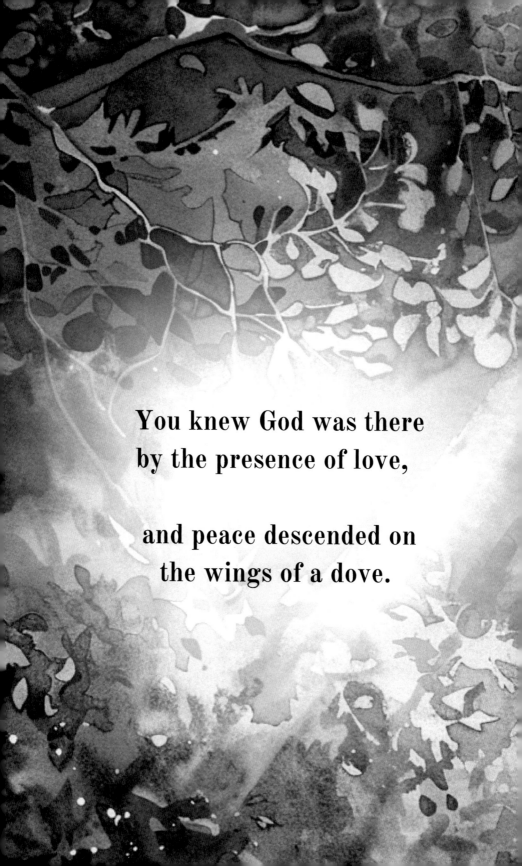

You knew God was there
by the presence of love,

and peace descended on
the wings of a dove.

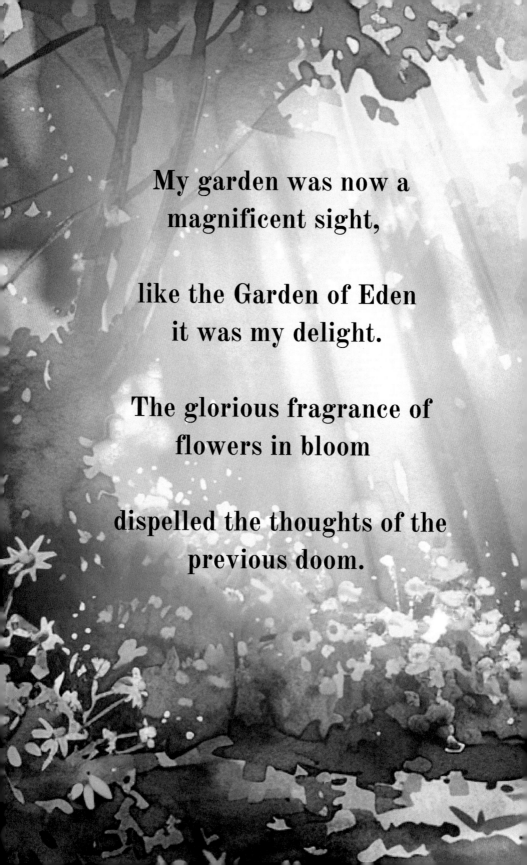

My garden was now a
magnificent sight,

like the Garden of Eden
it was my delight.

The glorious fragrance of
flowers in bloom

dispelled the thoughts of the
previous doom.

No one could love my
garden more
than the Gardener of Love
who came to restore.

The debt that I owe Him
can never be paid.

So, my life and my Garden
at His feet I have laid.

And they will say, "This land that was desolate has become like the garden of Eden, and the waste and desolate and ruined cities are now fortified and inhabited."

Ezekiel: 36:35 NASB

"When this is all over," Judah answers, "The tyrant toppled, the killing at an end, all signs of these cruelties long gone, a new government of love will be established in the venerable David tradition.
A Ruler you can depend upon will head this government, a Ruler passionate for justice, a Ruler quick to set things right."

Isaiah 16:4-5 MSG

The Gardener of Love:
A Journey from Despair to Renewal

Before becoming Program Director for the Clinical Psychiatric Unit's Christian Therapy Hospital Program, I was a group facilitator. These groups were the core of our program and served as the starting point for many patients' healing journeys.

We held a two-hour process group daily, helping patients work through intense emotions such as grief, rage, depression, anxiety, fear, sexual abuse, and other traumas.

These overwhelming emotions often led people to seek help from our program. It's common for people to feel hesitant about seeking help when they're struggling.

Overcoming the fear of the unknown is a big step, especially when entering a locked psychiatric unit, whether it's a Christian program or not.

As the group facilitator, I implemented warm-up exercises at the beginning of each session to promote interaction and make participants feel more comfortable.

Establishing trust within the group was crucial as it created a sense of security, which allowed them to share their feelings and experiences. Our groups were dynamic, consisting of 20-35 patients at any given time, each dealing with unique issues.

During our process groups, patients had the opportunity to release their deepest emotions through various therapeutic interventions, leading to breakthroughs and beautiful transformations. These sessions helped build a strong bond among the group as they supported each other and dealt with their painful issues.

The fear of judgment gave way to compassion, and shame gave way to a liberating new freedom. Together, we faced the pains and lifted each other's burdens, fulfilling the law of Christ as stated in Galatians 6:2.

One day, I observed patients entering the room. They were laughing and chatting about their breakthroughs in the group and what they wanted to work on during the session.

It was fascinating to see their physical change. Their faces were brighter, and their smiles were genuine. They joked as if they had known each other for years.

As they settled into their seats, I decided to share my observations. "Who are you?" I asked, to their surprise. They exchanged puzzled glances. "Who are you?" I repeated, then laughed, breaking the confusion.

"I don't recognize any of you anymore. You don't look like the same people who came here a few weeks ago." I continued, "When you checked in, you were so discouraged you couldn't even look at each other. Your faces were filled with despair and nearly distorted from your pain." They began to smile, recognizing the truth in my words.

"You were like a garden of beautiful flowers crushed and trampled into the ground by the enemy of your soul." I saw them nodding, understanding the metaphor. "But now, watching you, your faces are completely different. There's a new freedom shining through you. There's a light that brightens your face. You're more at ease with yourselves." Like a gardener, God showered His love upon His crushed garden, causing His flowers to bloom again.

"I am so proud of you for all your hard work. God met you at your point of need, and He is restoring your lives. He is so faithful." Tears filled my eyes as God's compassion flowed through me for His precious children. He is the Gardener of Love and Justice in an often unjust world.

This experience inspired me to write "The Garden." I wanted to capture the essence of God's active involvement in our lives, tending to the damaged places in our souls and bringing healing.

Through my Poem and its accompanying watercolor illustrations, I want to connect you to a personal vision of a loving Savior who loves you more than you know. He is your liberator, your Healer, and your soon-coming King.

PRAYER

Dear Heavenly Father,

We come before You with grateful hearts, acknowledging Your gracious love and mercy.

Thank You for being the Gardener of our souls and tending to those crushed places with Your gentle touch.

We ask for Your continued presence in our lives, guiding us through our darkest moments and bringing us into the light of Your love. Help us to trust in Your faithfulness and to see the beauty You are cultivating within us, even when we feel the pain of being trampled.

Renew our spirits and restore our hope that we may blossom into the fullness of the life You have planned for us. In Jesus' name, we pray.

Amen

REFLECTION

Take a moment to reflect on the patient's journey in the group. Consider the transformation from despair to hope, from darkness to light.

This change didn't happen overnight; it was a process of risking, sharing burdens, and allowing the tender love of God to heal the deep wounds.

Reflect on your own life.

Are there areas where you feel trampled and crushed?

Are there parts of your heart that need the Gardeners restorative touch?

Remember that God is faithful. He meets us at our point of need and brings healing. Reflect on His promises and trust that He is at work in your life, even when you can't see it.

ACTIVATION

To embed this truth in your heart, take a practical step towards restoration:

Create a Gratitude Journal: Write down three things you are grateful for daily. This practice shifts your focus from what is damaged to what is being restored. It helps you see the small ways God works in your life.

Spend Time in Nature: Go for a walk in a garden or park. Observe the flowers and plants. Notice how they grow and bloom despite the elements. Let this be a visual reminder of God's work in your life. Just as He tends to the garden, He is tending to you.

Reach Out to a Friend: Share your burdens with someone you trust. Allow them to support you and pray for you. Connection and community are vital parts of the healing process, just as they were for the patients in the group.

By incorporating these actions into your life, you can reinforce the truth of God's faithfulness and His role as the Gardener of your soul, nurturing you back to life.

ABOUT THE AUTHOR

Pamela Rice is a seasoned Marriage and Family Therapist with a Doctor of Ministry in applied theology. Based in Los Angeles, California, she offers a unique blend of clinical expertise and spiritual insight through her private practice.

Her personal journey through healing fuels her belief in the transformative power of faith. Pam is dedicated to helping others rebuild their lives and rediscover hope.

Beyond her professional life, Pam finds joy in nature and treasures her barefoot walks on the beach at twilight, "This is where the majesty of God puts life's challenges into perspective."

For more about Pam and her inspirational journey, visit her website at pamelaannrice.com. Her award-winning memoir, "Tarnished Crowns: A Memoir - The Power of Purpose and Authenticity," is available on Amazon.

TARNISHED CROWNS

A Memoir

The Power of Purpose and Authenticity

PAMELA ANN RICE

62370484R00048